MG - 6.4-1.0 pts

Artificial Intelligence

CHERRY LAKE PUBLISHING • ANN ARBOR, MICHIGAN

by Josh Gregory

A Note to Adults: Please review the instructions for the activities in this book before allowing children to do them. Be sure to help them with any activities you do not think they can safely complete on their own.

A Note to Kids: Be sure to ask an adult for help with these activities when you need it. Always put your safety first!

Published in the United States of America by Cherry Lake Publishing
Ann Arbor, Michigan
www.cherrylakepublishing.com

Content Adviser: Matthew Lammi, Assistant Professor of Technology,
Engineering & Design Education, North Carolina State University
Reading Adviser: Marla Conn MS, Ed., Literacy Specialist, Read-Ability, Inc.
Photo Credits: Cover and page 1, ©iurii/Shutterstock; page 4, ©Monkey Business Images/Dreamstime.com; page 7, ©Rocketclips, Inc./Dreamstime.com; page 8, ©B Christopher/Alamy Stock Photo; page 10, ©Heritage Image Partnership Ltd/Alamy Stock Photo; pages 13 and 17, ©ASSOCIATED PRESS; page 14, ©Diego Grandi/Shutterstock; page 19, ©Peppinuzzo/Shutterstock; page 21, ©Federico Rostagno/Shutterstock; page 22, ©catwalker/Shutterstock; page 24, ©Tom Wang/Shutterstock; page 25, ©dpa picture alliance/Alamy Stock Photo; page 27, ©Monkey Business Images/Shutterstock; page 28, ©aberCPC/Alamy Stock Photo

Library of Congress Cataloging-in-Publication Data has been filed and is available at catalog.loc.gov

Cherry Lake Publishing would like to acknowledge the work of the Partnership for 21st Century Learning. Please visit www.p21.org for more information.

Printed in the United States of America
Corporate Graphics

21st Century Skills INNOVATION LIBRARY

Contents

Chapter 1

Machines That Think

We use the word *intelligent* in many ways. A smart person can be described as intelligent. So can a clever pet that has learned to perform a trick. If you are watching a sci-fi movie, you might hear the characters talk about searching for "intelligent life" on a distant planet. You know that intelligence has something to do with thinking. But

Learning how to play a musical instrument requires a great deal of intelligence.

what exactly does it mean? Are all people intelligent? Are all animals? What about computers?

Intelligence is more than just being able to think or react to things. Experts define it as a blend of several abilities. One is perception, or the ability to absorb information about your surroundings. For a human, this means being able to recognize and make sense of the things you see, hear, feel, smell, or taste. Another part of intelligence is being able to learn new things. This could be as simple as remembering facts. It could also be as complex as learning to play an instrument or mastering a dance move.

Intelligence also means being able to reason. This means using the information you know to draw conclusions and learn new things. Problem solving is another big part of intelligence. If you find yourself in an unfamiliar situation, you can use your knowledge and skills to find a solution. Finally, intelligence means being able to understand and use language.

As you have used computers or played with robots, you have probably noticed that they seem to show some signs of intelligence. You might talk to your smartphone and ask it to look something up online for

Building a Brain

Scientists have been studying the human brain for centuries trying to understand how it works. While they still have a lot to learn, they do know the basic structure that makes the brain function. A human brain is made up of billions of special **cells** called **neurons**. Each neuron is connected to thousands of others. These connections form a massive, extremely complex web. The neurons can send electrical and chemical signals to each other. This is what makes the brain work.

One type of AI involves building computer systems that mimic this brain structure. This type of AI is called a neural network. A neural network is made up of many connected units. Each one functions much like a neuron. Neural networks are very good at finding patterns in large amounts of data. They have been used for everything from making predictions about the economy to creating weather forecasts.

you. You might also find that it learns how to spell your friends' names the more you type them. These are examples of something called artificial intelligence, or AI.

What makes your phone's intelligence artificial? After all, it seems to meet the definitions of intelligence. It hears your voice, it learns new things, and it even speaks the same language you do. However, computers cannot think and process information the same way people do. (Or at least, not yet.) Instead, they follow computer programs that are designed to imitate human intelligence.

The field of AI technology is based on searching for new ways to give machines and computers the abilities associated with intelligence. AI experts hope that one day, they will create a computer that has a mind of its own and is just as intelligent as a human. That day could be long off in the future, and

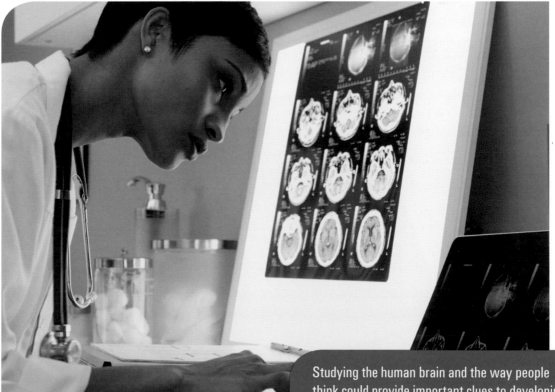

Studying the human brain and the way people think could provide important clues to developing better AI technology.

it may never come at all. But in the meantime, AI will continue to get better and better.

Although today's AI technology has limitations, it is already quite impressive in many ways. Computers can perceive their environments using **sensors** and cameras. They can even **analyze** what they are "seeing." For example, researchers built one AI that could look at photographs and figure out whether there were any cats in the pictures.

AI programs power the technology that allows you to talk to your smartphone and ask it questions.

Modern computers can be taught new things by feeding them information or through using trial and error. They can reason by using complex math to process different kinds of information. They can use their programming to solve many kinds of problems. They can even understand and use some parts of human language, both written and spoken.

Despite already having a rich and fascinating history, AI is in many ways still a developing field. Even though researchers have made huge breakthroughs over the years, they still have a long way to go before they create a truly intelligent machine. Many basic concepts of AI are uncertain. For example, experts do not always agree about the best way to develop new AI systems. Some think the way forward lies in creating faster computers and more complex programs. Others believe it is better to study the structure of the human brain and use this knowledge to build artificial "brains."

Chapter 2

From Theory to Reality

People have wondered for centuries what makes our minds work. Throughout history, scientists, doctors, and other researchers have studied how people think, learn, solve problems, and communicate.

Alan Turing was one of the earliest researchers to pursue the idea of building machines that could think for themselves.

Over time, they developed countless theories and learned a great deal about intelligence.

By the early 20th century, technology was advancing at an incredible pace. Inventions such as the automobile and the television were changing the way people lived. Innovators were working on projects that would lead to the creation of the first robots and computers. With all of the excitement around new technology, some people began to speculate about the possibility of machines that could think for themselves.

In 1935, a British mathematician named Alan Turing wrote of his ideas for a machine that could store information in a memory bank and then use that information later to complete tasks. This marked the beginning of the modern era of artificial intelligence.

Turing continued to play a major role in pushing AI and computer technology forward. During World War II (1939–1945), the British government hired Turing and other mathematicians as code breakers. The country's enemies in Germany were using a device called an Enigma machine to **encrypt** their messages. The machine's settings were changed

Turing's Test

One of Alan Turing's most enduring contributions to the study of AI is a test he designed to determine whether a machine is truly intelligent. To perform the test, a human "interrogator" sits at a computer and types questions. He or she receives responses from two other users. One is an AI program, and the other is human. The interrogator has to decide which one is which.

During the test, the AI is allowed to do whatever it takes to convince the interrogator it is human. This includes lying or intentionally answering questions wrong. If the interrogator cannot tell which user is human and which is an AI program, then the AI has passed the test.

Today, the Turing Test, as it is known, remains an important concept in AI studies. So far, no AI has ever been able to pass it.

every day. This meant the code breakers only had 24 hours to break each code before it changed again. Even for some of the world's most skilled mathematicians, it wasn't enough time.

Turing and his colleagues solved this problem by building an electronic machine that could crack the codes faster than any human. With the device's help, Great Britain learned about Germany's plans ahead of time. This saved many lives and helped end the war.

After the war, Turing continued to study computers and AI. His ideas and writings inspired many other

John McCarthy sets up a game board during a test of a chess-playing AI program.

people to begin AI projects of their own. For example, in 1951, an inventor named Christopher Strachey created a computer program that could play checkers. His creation was improved even further by another inventor named Arthur Samuel. By 1955, Samuel had created a version of the program that could learn and improve over time.

That same year, the term *artificial intelligence* was used for the first time. Scientist John McCarthy coined the term while organizing a conference to be held in

The Massachusetts Institute of Technology was the center of many major AI breakthroughs.

1956 at Dartmouth College in New Hampshire. There, McCarthy and many other scientists and mathematicians gathered to discuss their ideas for creating computers that could think for themselves.

For several weeks, McCarthy and his colleagues brainstormed and debated the possibilities of AI projects. Many of the event's attendees went on to become leaders in the field. For example, Marvin Minsky joined with McCarthy to start an AI lab at the Massachusetts Institute of Technology (MIT). The lab remains an important hub of AI research even today.

Dartmouth workshop attendees Allen Newell and Herbert Simon joined with computer programmer J. Clifford Shaw in 1956 to create a groundbreaking program called Logic Theorist. Considered one of the first true AI programs, it was able to prove extremely complex mathematics theories that humans had struggled with for decades. All three creators went on to create other important AI programs.

AI research continued to draw a great deal of attention during the 1960s. In 1960, McCarthy created a computer programming language designed mainly for creating AI programs. Called LISP (short for "list processing"), it remains an important tool of AI programmers even today.

In 1966, researchers at the MIT AI lab showed off computer programs designed to imitate human conversations. Users could type questions to one of two different computer personalities. The programs would respond using a variety of preprogrammed answers. Though they were not truly intelligent, these programs helped show the way forward for similar AI personalities.

By the 1970s, huge advances in computer technology were happening all the time. In the 1960s, most computers were enormous and very expensive. They were used mainly by governments and researchers. But by the beginning of the 1980s, that had all changed. Personal computers were widely available. Many businesses had started using computer systems to make their operations more **efficient**.

This widespread use of computers inspired a demand for AI-based programs that could help businesses. Programmers created AI software to do everything from creating schedules to analyzing financial data. These AI programs could be both faster and more accurate than human workers. This trend has continued over time, with AI programs taking over many jobs from humans even today.

Over the years, AI technology has improved in many ways. In 2011, an AI program called Watson competed on the popular TV game show *Jeopardy!* Watson faced off against two of the biggest winners in the quiz show's history and came out on top. Its victory was based on a lot more than just knowing trivia. The show's questions are often designed to be tricky. They sometimes require players to think in creative ways. This didn't stop Watson. The AI program had trained

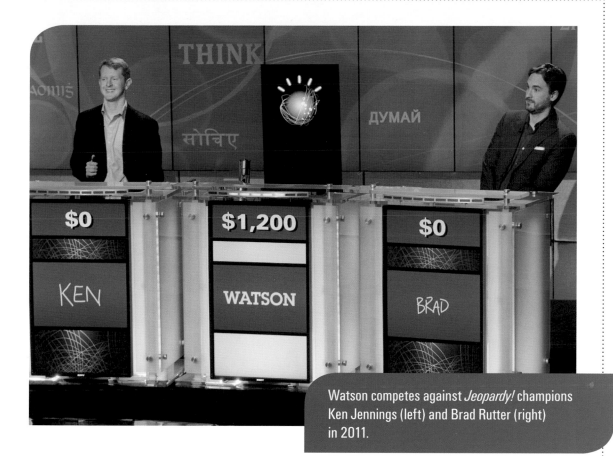

Watson competes against *Jeopardy!* champions Ken Jennings (left) and Brad Rutter (right) in 2011.

for three years to recognize different types of questions and determine exactly what was being asked.

The software behind Watson is now being used for everything from health care to weather forecasts. And while its accomplishments are certainly impressive, it is still only the tip of the iceberg of what AI is capable of doing.

Chapter 3

AI Today

We still have a long way to go before we see the creation of a truly intelligent computer. However, the AI technology we already have is being used in many interesting ways today. In fact, you probably interact with AI systems almost every day without thinking about it.

Some of the most popular AI programs today are the digital assistants that are built into our phones, tablets, computers, and other devices. These include Apple's Siri, Amazon's Alexa, Microsoft's Cortana, and Google's "OK Google" voice detection. Each of these programs is slightly different, but they are all based on the same basic idea. You can simply talk to your electronic devices and ask them to do things for you. They can search the Internet for information, set reminders, or place orders from online stores. They can even control the lighting, temperature, and other features of your home. All you have to do is talk out loud and ask them to do what you want.

This trend got off to a start in 2008, when Google first released its speech recognition app for the

Devices such as the Amazon Echo allow users to interact with AI programs using spoken conversation.

iPhone. At the time, researchers had been working for decades to create AIs that understood spoken language. However, all those years of work had led to a system that was only able to understand what people were saying about 80 percent of the time.

Google's new app was designed not only to be useful, but to make speech recognition work better. Every time someone uses the app, Google collects the voice recordings. This data is passed through huge neural networks designed to recognize patterns

Fiction or Future?

The possibilities of artificial intelligence have long inspired writers, filmmakers, and other storytellers. In turn, their creations have motivated innovative thinkers to pursue new AI projects that could live up to their favorite stories. Author Isaac Asimov's 1950 short story collection *I, Robot* was one early inspiration. Before the term *artificial intelligence* had even been coined, Asimov's stories dealt with the potential difficulties that would arise when humans interacted with AI-powered robots.

in human speech. The system learns more and more about the way people talk. This leads it to become better at understanding. As a result, Google's speech recognition software has improved very quickly. The company claims that it is now about 92 percent accurate. Newer programs, such as Siri, are even better, with accuracy up to 95 percent.

Another way you might encounter AI is by playing your favorite video games. Any time you play against a computer instead of a human, you are

You interact with an AI program every time you play a single-player video game.

playing against an AI program. Early video game AI might have been as simple as a computer program that told an enemy to move from left to right over and over again. But today's games feature complex AI enemies that play like humans. They can predict your movements and pull off tricky strategies. In some cases, they are good enough to pose a challenge for even the most skilled human players.

AI also plays an important role in the creation of robots. From small automatic vacuum cleaners that search out stray crumbs to advanced robots that can walk and talk like people, they all depend on AI programs to tell them how to behave. Self-driving cars, another rapidly advancing form of technology, also rely on AI to help them navigate and avoid collisions.

Not every AI does something you can see. Sometimes AI programs are hard at work behind the scenes. For example, AI is used to help improve

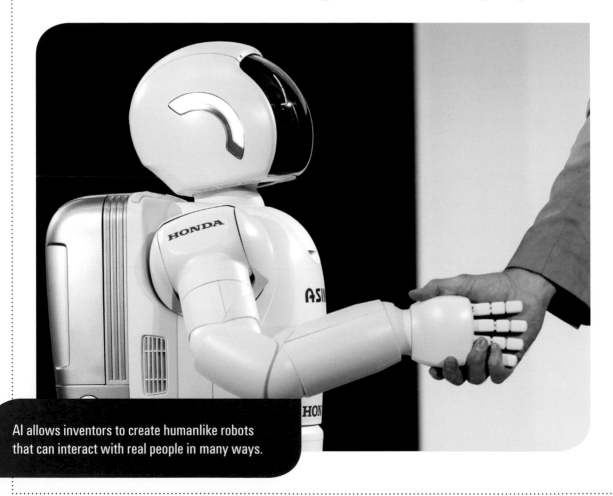

AI allows inventors to create humanlike robots that can interact with real people in many ways.

search engine results. Every time you type a word or phrase into Google, the search engine's neural networks absorb the information. They also pay attention to what you are clicking on. This information helps the systems figure out what people are really searching for when they type in certain groups of words. This allows Google to provide the most relevant links to each user. Like speech recognition programs, the search engines are able to learn and get better over time.

Chapter 4

Thinking for Themselves

A s time goes on, AI is likely to become more and more common in our everyday lives. Even today, AI technology is being used in many more ways than it was just a few short years ago. The continued improvement and wider use of AI will lead

As AI technology becomes more and more common, it will affect many people's everyday lives.

to exciting possibilities. At the same time, it could create new problems for people. For example, if AI programs continue to take over jobs at their current rate, what will humans do for work? How will it change the economy?

Another issue involves how to control the way AI programs make certain decisions. For example, think about a self-driving car. The AI that operates the car is programmed to avoid hitting pedestrians. It is also

Self-driving cars such as the ones built by Google will raise new questions about AI technology.

The Singularity

AI experts often spend time imagining what the future could be like if certain technology was created. One thing they have long considered is what would happen if an AI became smart enough to make improvements to itself or even create its own AI programs. They call this potential event "the Singularity." They believe that if the Singularity occurred, the AI would very quickly grow more intelligent than any human. It would potentially be able to do things that humans cannot even predict or understand. Some people fear that this would lead to the end of life as we know it. Others believe that the Singularity is an impossible situation that will never come true. Either way, it probably won't be happening anytime soon. After all, there is still no proof that an AI can be as intelligent as a human.

programmed to keep its passengers safe and avoid swerving off the road. But what if it is in a situation where the only two choices are to hit a pedestrian or swerve into a wall? Either situation involves someone getting hurt or possibly even killed. How does the AI decide what to do? These are questions AI programmers will have to consider carefully as AI takes on more important roles in our everyday lives.

One big question is whether it will be possible to create a truly intelligent AI system that can think for itself and make all of its own decisions. The AI programs we use today are categorized as specific AIs. This means they only know how to do specific things.

Human drivers can make split-second life-or-death decisions that AIs are not capable of.

But AI inventors have long dreamed of creating a generalized AI program. This is a program with a mind of its own. It would be able to learn new information and skills just like people do. It would also be able to interact with humans and carry on conversations.

If such an AI were created, it would introduce many **moral** questions. Should a fully intelligent AI receive the same rights as a human? Would deactivating the AI be considered murder? Or what if the AI decided to hurt someone or commit a crime? Would

Programmers, engineers, and other tech innovators will continue to push AI technology forward in the future.

its creators be responsible? AI experts often ask
these kinds of questions as they ponder the future of
their field. But even with these serious issues on their
minds, they remain excited about the future. No one
knows for sure where AI technology will take us, but
the process of finding out is sure to be a thrilling ride.

Glossary

analyze (AN-uh-lize) to examine something carefully to understand it

cells (SEHLZ) the smallest whole parts in plants and animals

efficient (ih-FISH-uhnt) working very well and not wasting time or money

encrypt (in-KRIPT) to change information from one form to another to hide its meaning

moral (MOR-uhl) concerned with right and wrong behavior

neurons (NOOR-ahnz) cells that carry information between the brain and other parts of the body

sensors (SEN-surz) instruments that detect and measure changes

Find Out More

BOOK

Gregory, Josh. *Robots.* Ann Arbor, MI: Cherry Lake Publishing, 2018.

WEB SITES

Association for the Advancement of Artificial Intelligence

www.aaai.org

Keep up with the latest advancements in AI technology.

BBC iWonder—Alan Turing: Creator of Modern Computing

www.bbc.co.uk/timelines/z8bgr82

Learn more about AI pioneer Alan Turing.

Index

About the Author

Josh Gregory is the author of more than 100 books for kids. He has written about everything from animals to technology to history. A graduate of the University of Missouri–Columbia, he currently lives in Portland, Oregon.